Kim

Care for your
Guinea
Pig

CONTENTS

Introduction	4
Varieties	6
Guinea pigs in South America	10
Biology	12
Choosing a guinea pig	14
Companionship	16
The hutch and enclosure	20
The grazing ark	22
Indoor exercising	24
Feeding	26
Cleaning the hutch	30
Grooming	32
Handling	33
The healthy guinea pig	34
When you are away	36
First aid	37
Ailments and parasites	38
Reproduction	40
The young	42
Your questions answered	44
Life history	46
Record card	47
Index	48

Collins

Published by William Collins Sons & Co Ltd
London · Glasgow · Sydney · Auckland · Toronto · Johannesburg

© Royal Society for the Prevention of Cruelty to Animals 1981, 1990

NEW EDITION

First published 1990

9 8 7 6 5 4 3 2

This is a fully revised and extended edition
of *Care for Your Guinea Pig*, first published in 1981
and reprinted 8 times

Text of the 1981 edition by Tina Hearne; text
revisions and additions for this edition by Margaret Crush

Designed and edited by Templar Publishing Ltd.,
Pippbrook Mill, Dorking, Surrey

Front cover photograph by Sue Streeter

Text photographs by Solitaire, Bruce Coleman Ltd *(also back cover, bottom)*,
Anne Cumbers, Dr. David Guiterman, Spectrum Colour Library Ltd, Sue Streeter
(also back cover, centre), Sally Ann Thompson, ZEFA

Illustrations by Terry Riley and Mike Woodhatch/David Lewis Artists, and
Bob Hersey/Bernard Thornton Artists

A catalogue record for this book is available from the British Library

Printed in Italy by New Interlitho, Milan

ISBN 0 00 412549 5

First things first, animals are fun. Anybody who has ever enjoyed the company of a pet knows well enough just how strong the bond between human and animal can be. Elderly or lonely people often depend on a pet for their only company, and this can be a rewarding relationship for both human and animal. Doctors have proved that animals can be instrumental in the prevention of and recovery from mental or physical disease. Children learn the meaning of loyalty, unselfishness and friendship by growing up with animals.

But the commitment to an animal doesn't begin and end with a visit to the local pet shop. It's a commitment for the whole of that animal's lifetime – anything up to 20 years of total responsibility for its health and well-being. If you are not prepared for the inevitable expense, time, patience and occasional frustration involved, then the RSPCA would much rather that you didn't have a pet.

Armed with the facts, aware of the pitfalls but still confident of your ability to give a pet a good home, the next step is to find where you can get an animal from. Seek the advice of a veterinary surgeon or RSPCA Inspector about reputable local breeders or suppliers. Do consider the possibility of offering a home to an animal from an RSPCA establishment. There are no animals more deserving of loving owners.

As for the care of your pet, you should find in the following pages all you need to know to keep it happy, healthy and rewarding for many years to come.

Responsible ownership means happy pets. Enjoy the experience!

DAVID WILKINS
Chief Veterinary Officer, RSPCA

Introduction

Guinea pigs, or cavies, are among the most popular of the pet rodents. They are docile with people, and soon become tame and tractable, while their size and shape allow them to be easily handled by children. Since they do not climb much and are not as agile as some of the smaller rodents, they present less of a worry than, say, hamsters or gerbils, should they run free.

GUINEA PIG OR CAVY?

The use of the word cavy when referring to these animals is scientifically correct, and is favoured by the fanciers who run Cavy Clubs throughout the country. The general public, however, still clings to the more popular guinea pig, and either name is acceptable.

The use of the word 'guinea', however, is curious, and has not been satisfactorily explained. There are several possibilities, and the most acceptable suggests that it is a corruption of Guiana. Originally guinea pigs were exported from the (then) Guiana coast of South America, from which the animals were first brought to Europe by Spanish sailors.

Cavia porcellus is the scientific name, meaning the 'pig-like cavy', and the smooth breeds, which are most like the wild cavies, do rather resemble pigs in outline. There is also a similarity of movement: sometimes, like pigs, these cavies 'trot', with the body lifted well clear of the ground, and moving more slowly than in their normal low, scurrying run.

THE RIGHT PET?

The guinea pig is a grassland animal by nature and is quite easy to care for when the right facilities are available. The short-haired breeds need little more than warm, dry accommodation, a good herbivorous diet, and regular access to a grazing and exercise area. Long-haired types have exotic appeal but of course need regular and frequent grooming.

This rough-haired Tortoiseshell and White may not be pure-bred and of show standard, but is just as appealing a pet.

In their native grasslands, guinea pigs live as social animals, in family colonies, and when kept as pets they should be housed together, if at all possible, in small compatible groups. For breeding purposes one male is usually kept with several females, but as pets it is recommended that two or more females be kept together. Adult males will usually not share accommodation without fighting.

Those deprived of the company of other guinea pigs will suffer from an unnatural isolation, and in particular circumstances the loss can even be physically harmful. A case in point is the problem of exposure. It sometimes happens, that an unexpected cold snap will take owners unawares, and guinea pigs will be found suffering from exposure, having been left in an unprotected hutch, perhaps with too small a quantity of bedding. In such circumstances, several guinea pigs would huddle together for warmth, and perhaps survive quite well; in very similar circumstances, a lone guinea pig could well succumb.

As guinea pigs are not hardy enough to endure draughts, damp and very cold weather, you will need to be able to provide extra shelter in the winter. A well-built shed or outbuilding will be suitable if it is warmed, when necessary, with a small heater such as those used for greenhouses and garages.

Warning When providing extra warmth in winter take care to ensure that there is sufficient ventilation without leaving your guinea pig in a draught. Paraffin heaters in particular can cause a dangerous build-up of fumes in an enclosed space.

Varieties

A domestic guinea pig is roughly the same size as its close relation, the wild cavy of Peru, though the latter has a more pointed, almost rat-like face and is speckled greyish brown in colour. When the first specimens of wild cavies were introduced into Europe towards the end of the sixteenth century, they rapidly became popular pets.

Today there are three major varieties of guinea pig, all of which are descended from a common ancestor. They are the short, smooth-coated breeds (called English, American or Bolivian); the harsh-coated, rosetted Abyssinians (though these animals certainly do not come from Africa); and the long-haired, silky-coated Peruvians.

Tortoiseshell and White

COLOUR VARIATIONS
Within these three main varieties are about 25 groupings of colours and markings, the result of skilled breeders taking guinea pigs with slight differences in colour and mating them to produce new colour variations. The science of genetics explains these variants.

In genetics each hereditary characteristic, such as colour, is determined by a pair of genes, one inherited from the male or boar guinea pig, the other from the female or sow. Two pure-bred black guinea pigs will produce offspring which are all black. But a pure-bred black guinea pig mated to a pure-bred white will pass on one black gene and one white, so the offspring may well be grey – a compromise between the colours they have inherited from their parents. Even if some of the young turn out, by chance, to be all black or all white, the next generation may not breed true.

Among guinea pig breeders, single-coloured guinea pigs are known as Selfs, and each colour is recognized as a separate breed: Self White, Self Black, Self Cream, Self Beige, Self Golden, Self Lilac, Self Red and Self Chocolate.

Other guinea pigs have two or more colours, and often distinct body markings. Such guinea pigs with two or more colours in a pattern are classified as Marked.

Self: Black

Golden Agouti

Some Marked combinations have special breed names, such as Dutch, Agouti, Tortoiseshell and Himalayan. Of these the **Dutch** is often seen, although those sold as pets are unlikely to have perfect markings. Breeders try to achieve an unbroken saddle band and a flash down the centre of the face in the basic white fur, separating the three dark areas – each side of the face and the hindquarters.

Abyssinian mother and young

Agouti guinea pigs are said to resemble the wild cavies more than any other breed. They have a pepper-and-salt effect that is the result of the hairs being tipped with black. There are Gold, Silver, Salmon, Lemon and Cinnamon Agoutis.

Tortoiseshell and **Tortoiseshell and White** are other favourite breeds. The coats are patterned with blocks of black and red (tortoiseshell), or black, red and white (tortoiseshell and white), of roughly equal size, arranged alternately on either side of the body.

Himalayan guinea pigs are marked like Siamese cats, although the young do not show the coloured points at birth. The points – ears, nose, and feet – become defined when the young guinea pig is five or six months old.

All short-haired and most rough-haired breeds can be found in all the Self colours and most of the Marked combinations.

Himalayan

SHORT-HAIRED BREEDS

The so-called **English, American** or **Bolivian** breeds are the easiest of all to groom, retaining the short, smooth coat of the wild cavies.

ROUGH-HAIRED BREED

During the long period of domestication certain mutations of coat type have occurred, and the rough-haired, or **Abyssinian**, is a particularly attractive example.

The hair of an Abyssinian is straight and coarse, and stands up to a height of 3 cm/1½ in all over the body, arranged in a pattern of rosettes, with a ridge along the spine. A show specimen would have ten rosettes: four around the saddle; two on each flank; and one on each shoulder.

Pet Abyssinians may show far less perfect markings, and many are the result of crossbreeding with smooth-haired guinea pigs, showing only a single rosette.

The Abyssinians occur in a range of Self colours, and also in the Marked colours, for instance, Agouti and Tortoiseshell.

Rough-haired: Tortoiseshell and White

LONG-HAIRED BREEDS

The **Peruvian**, whose long, silky hair may well grow to floor length, or even longer in show specimens, is the best-known of the long-haired breeds. Fanciers frequently keep Peruvians with their long hair rolled up in paper curlers between shows. The hair falls towards the floor from a parting along the back, and covers the face. Obviously this is a variety for the show bench rather than for the garden enclosure, as it requires daily grooming.

More recent long-haired breeds are the **Sheltie**, similar to the Peruvian, but with hair growing back off the face in a long mane, and the **Coronet**, which looks just like the Sheltie, but with a crest or rosette on the head.

The best place to acquire a good specimen guinea pig for showing is from a reputable breeder. Often such people will be exhibiting at local Rabbit and Cavy Club shows, or the secretary of the National Cavy Club will forward a list of breeders in the area.

Pure-bred varieties are kept primarily for show purposes, but the vast majority of guinea pigs bought as pets are a mixture of two or more varieties. Provided they are healthy, cross-bred guinea pigs make good pets.

Long-haired: Peruvian

Guinea pigs in South America

Several different species of cavy are still to be found in their native South America.

The wild ancestor of the domesticated guinea pig, *Cavia porcellus*, is thought to be the restless cavy, *Cavia cutleri*. This particular cavy is native to Peru, where it is a grazing animal, almost entirely dependent on grass for both food and shelter.

The restless cavies live in extended family groups in surface runs trodden through long grass, and protected above by the overhanging stems. The cavies may use rock crevices or the abandoned burrows of other animals, but as far as is known they do not excavate for themselves. They can be attacked by larger, meat-eating enemies, so they are rather timid and hide quickly when frightened.

Young cavies are not born in a safe burrow, but in the open, so they must be able to look after themselves almost as soon as they are born. Consequently, they arrive fully furred, with their eyes already open. Two days after being born, they start eating the same food as their parents.

Before the Spanish conquest of South America in the sixteenth century the Incas kept these animals for food, and even today the Peruvians breed them for the table, rather as certain breeds of rabbit are sometimes kept for their meat in Britain. Sailors were probably the first to keep cavies exclusively as pets, and introduce them to Europe from South America.

Biology

Rodents The guinea pigs belong to the order of rodents, the gnawing animals, which must constantly wear down their continuously growing teeth or face starvation. This may happen because the jaws can no longer close, or perhaps because one unopposed incisor tooth grows until it locks into its opposite jaw, and so clamps both together (see Teeth).

The rodents themselves, which comprise the largest and most widespread order of mammals on earth are divided into three sub-orders: *Sciuromorpha* (squirrels, and beavers); *Myomorpha* (mice, rats, and hamsters); and *Hystricomorpha* (cavies, coypu, porcupines, and chinchilla).

The hystricomorphs are all native to the one geographical area of South America, Central America and the Caribbean Islands, and it is to this sub-order that the guinea pigs and all the cavies belong.

They have characteristically very long pregnancies, and consequently precocious young born with fur, teeth and open eyes. They are able to withstand surface life from the first day.

Many hystricomorphs have pregnancies of one hundred days or more. Guinea pigs have a pregnancy period of about 63 days, which is comparable to that of cats and dogs, and is much longer than the average gestation of the other major pet rodents: rabbit (31 days), gerbil (24 days), rat (22 days), mouse (21 days), golden hamster (16 days).

Teeth The cheek teeth as well as the front incisor teeth grow continuously, and have to be worn down by constant wear. In contrast to rabbits, which use a side-to-side movement when chewing, guinea pigs grind food from front to back, and hay, raw vegetables and hard fruit all help to keep the teeth in trim. In addition, guinea pigs need a gnawing block. A freshly cut log with the bark left on is best, but avoid those from poisonous trees such as yew and laburnum.

Like all rodents, guinea pigs have a gap called a diastema where a carnivore would have canine teeth or premolars. The diastema enables the rodent to draw in its cheeks and close off the rest of the mouth, so it does not swallow injurious material while gnawing at bark, etc.

At birth guinea pigs have their full set of teeth. Any difficulty with feeding may point to some abnormality in their dentition, generally overgrowth of the incisors, needing professional trimming.

Voice Guinea pigs have a whole range of vocal noises, of which the most often heard is an insistent 'wee-wee-wee' sound. Others include grunts, squeaks, chatterings, and chirrupings, so that at different times one may imagine they sound like a variety of other mammals, and quite often like birds.

Claws In the wild the claws are worn down continually as the guinea pigs constantly move across rough ground in order to graze. In captivity the four claws of each forefoot and the three of each hindfoot need to be worn down naturally, if possible, by exercising and grazing on the ground. When conditions are too soft to provide enough friction, or when the animals are kept for long periods on soft floor litter, or on deep straw the claws may become overgrown and need trimming (see p.35).

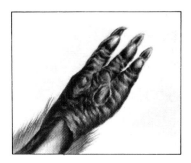

Lack of tail An animal's tail may have many useful functions: to act as a support, balance, and rudder; to be a muffler, or fly swat; to store fat for the winter; even, among prehensile animals, to serve as another limb. When an animal like the guinea pig has no apparent tail we have to accept that it serves no biological purpose and the appendage has been lost through the long process of evolution.

Many people believe that guinea pigs have no tails at all. In fact, a guinea pig does have a tail – but one so short that it does not project outside the body. The last five or seven caudal vertebrae can be felt underneath the skin at the base of the spine, but all that shows externally is a slight, round depression.

Choosing a guinea pig

The following points should be considered before falling for a cuddly little guinea pig in the pet shop.

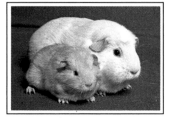

Children are able to lift guinea pigs with confidence. The average weight is about 900 g/ 2 lb, and the little animals seldom struggle when handled.

Age   Young guinea pigs should be fully weaned and are best bought between six and twelve weeks of age. At this age they are well able to look after themselves without their mother, yet are young enough to be easily tamed, provided they are handled frequently and gently.

Health   Guinea pigs should be healthy, so their owner will get the utmost enjoyment from them and not be dogged by worry or veterinary bills. Anyone selling a guinea pig should let the purchaser handle it to check over the following points (see also p.35).

A six-week-old guinea pig should weigh about 250 g/ 8½ oz, with a plump, well-fed body. The coat should be sleek, with the hairs sticking neither up nor out unless the animal is an Abyssinian. The fur should have some shine to it, even if the guinea pig is a rough-haired breed, and there should be no bald patches. The skin should be smooth, not dry, with no scaly areas, visible wounds, sores or abscesses. There should be no signs of nasal discharge or diarrhoea, the ears should be clean, the eyes bright, and the teeth clean and not overlong.

The guinea pig should walk or run smoothly, without any sign of lameness, and have an alert, confident appearance. It should be bold enough to be enticed to the front of the hutch with a titbit, or just to smell a finger. Taking the titbit will also confirm that the animal has a healthy appetite.

By holding the guinea pig close, it should be possible to check for noisy breathing: a guinea pig that wheezes is in poor health.

Breed   Unless the guinea pigs are wanted for showing, cross-breds will do very well for pets. However, it is important that a cross-bred be healthy. Many cross-bred guinea pigs are available simply because they do not meet the stringent requirements of the breed but unfortunately others may have been bred from old, immature or underfed stock, and consequently be small and frail.

For a first venture into keeping guinea pigs, a smooth-haired breed is probably best. Rough-haired guinea pigs need grooming every day, and long-haired Peruvians are definitely not for beginners.

Sources Many pet shops sell cross-breds, or a friend or acquaintance may have surplus guinea pigs and be pleased to find them a good home. However, top quality show guinea pigs will have to be purchased from a specialist breeder (see p.9).

Sexing Guinea pigs may be sexed if cradled in the crook of the handler's arm so that the genital opening is accessible. Gentle pressure around the opening will show up the Y-shaped slit of the female, and will extrude the penis of the male. The presence of nipples is no indication of sex in guinea pigs. Both males and females have two, positioned low down on the abdomen. The males may also be expected to be larger than the females right from birth.

Even pet shop owners have been known to make mistakes in sexing an animal, so it is a wise precaution to double check for yourself.

Genital openings of guinea pigs. Left: Male showing extruded penis. Right: Female showing divided Y-shaped slit.

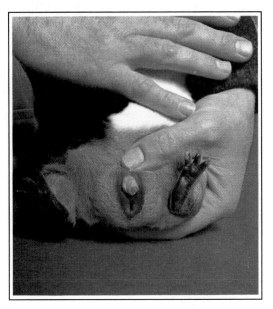

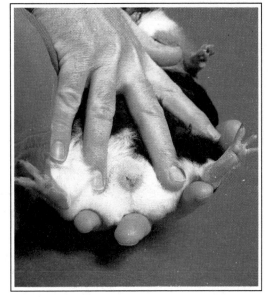

Companionship

It is very unkind to keep a pet guinea pig on its own – the animal is unlikely to be happy or to thrive. It is best to keep at least two guinea pigs, remembering that two animals are only marginally more trouble than one. Unless a pair is needed for breeding (see p.40), two young litter mates of the same sex should be chosen, or a father and son, or mother and daughter.

Two adult guinea pigs of the same sex not reared together should never be mixed, unless they can have an infinitely greater amount of space than the average garden enclosure can offer. They will almost certainly fight, especially if they are two males, which are more assertive in temperament than females. Not all females are docile. Some highly strung individuals may be too aggressive to live with other females, and any female may turn on a male if unwilling to be mated.

If, for some reason it is impossible to keep two guinea pigs, a guinea pig on its own will definitely need other companionship, since its owner is unlikely to be able to spend sufficient time with it. A small to medium-sized rabbit is a good companion, providing the animals are introduced when young. Even unlikely-looking companions like tortoises and poultry are better than solitude.

INTRODUCING THE PET

The hutch should be prepared before the guinea pigs are brought home. Let them run by themselves, that is, without being lifted, from the carrying container into the hutch, and allow them to settle in for a few days before letting family and friends view them. Cats and dogs should also be kept well out of the way.

Once they are used to their new home, do not drag them out screaming (and guinea pigs are very vocal in complaint). Stroke them gently with one finger while they are still in the hutch and eating. When they get used to this, use the whole hand for stroking and gradually accustom them to being lifted.

Tortoiseshell-coloured Abyssinian with young rabbit

Rough-haired Tortoiseshell and White with young

Peruvian

Peruvian

Bolivian

The hutch and enclosure

The inside of the hutch needs to have containers for food and water, a rack for hay, a layer of newspaper under a layer of peatmoss or other suitable floor litter, together with a generous quantity of hay or oat straw for the bedding compartment. If there is a roof overhang at the front of the hutch, the interior will be far better protected in wet weather.

Guinea pigs need a sturdy hutch, similar in design to that used for rabbits. Some hutches, which are rather too cramped for any but the smallest rabbit breeds, provide good accommodation for guinea pigs.

Two communicating compartments are recommended. One should have a wire-mesh front, admitting enough light to make the compartment suitable for daytime use and, in particular, for feeding. The other needs a solid front so that it provides a dark, sheltered retreat for daytime rest periods and for night use. Guinea pigs do not always choose to sleep in their 'bedroom' and prefer to camp out in the living area. After their routine has been watched for a few days, put the bedding where the animals decide to sleep.

If the fronts are made as two hinged doors, then there is

easy access to every part of the interior and cleaning is made simple (pp.30-1).

The hutch must be raised off the ground, well clear of rising damp and must be weatherproof. On cold or stormy days, and during firework displays, a louvred panel can be clipped to the front of the hutch. Polythene sheeting can also provide some protection provided there is sufficient ventilation.

During most of the year the hutch may be stood in an enclosure so that, in the daytime, the guinea pigs' accommodation can be extended by the use of a ramp.

Rocky caves, a log placed over a scrape of earth, drain-pipes, piles of hay, and the hutch itself provide the cover these animals are so quick to seek. If there is any danger of attack from cats or dogs, then a cover of wire mesh stretched on a wooden frame must be used over the entire enclosure.

In very cold weather the guinea pigs will be at risk if left in an exposed hutch, even if provided with plenty of bedding straw. As temperatures begin to fall, the hutch must be moved into the house, or into the shelter of a good shed or outbuilding.

A roomy enclosure with access to shelter allows guinea pigs freedom with maximum security. A mesh cover may be needed for protection from dogs and cats, and to keep sparrows from taking all the grain. At night the ramp should be removed and the guinea pigs shut up in the hutch which must be fitted with good safety catches or bolts.

The grazing ark

Wire netting could cause sore feet and so an ark is better without a mesh floor if it is to be used exclusively for guinea pigs, which make no attempt to escape by burrowing. If the base frame is well made, and sturdy enough to rest squarely on flat ground, then there is no danger that the guinea pigs will be able to crawl out from underneath.

An ark is for temporary use and not a substitute for a hutch, but it is vital that it provides a sheltered area, with hay for cover, which may be used as a retreat from any disturbance, or from rain and cold. Placing the ark partly in the shade of trees or buildings in summer will prevent its occupants from overheating, to which guinea pigs are very prone (see p.37).

Guinea pigs kept in a hutch without an enclosure need a portable ark for both grazing and exercise. Those which do have a permanent enclosure (pp.20-1) would also benefit by having an ark in which they can feed naturally outside during part of the day. By using an ark that is frequently moved on to fresh grass, guinea pigs are able to satisfy their very basic need to graze.

Indoor exercising

An indoor play pen is ideal for those days when the weather is too wet, or too harsh, for guinea pigs to graze and exercise in the open air.

They have the same active quality that gives their ancestral species its name – the restless cavy – and they should not be shut in a hutch for long periods, but given opportunity to exercise even when the grazing area cannot be used.

Many owners are prepared to allow their guinea pigs some freedom in the house, but they tend to gnaw electric cables and the like, and may be safer in a play pen. Also, although many guinea pigs do use just one area for their droppings, others are less discriminating.

An indoor play pen is suitable for exercising guinea pigs in cold or damp weather when they would be at risk or uncomfortable outside.

The most convenient indoor exercise area, as in the illustration, is a large, shallow-sided tray that can be cleaned out easily with a dustpan and brush. If the play pen is mounted on runners or castors, it can be easily pushed aside when the room has to be cleaned.

An area of around 1 m sq/3 ft sq for one guinea pig, 4 m sq/12 ft sq for two or three, would be ideal, but equally important is an *interesting* play area. A compact pen, but with hidey-holes and branches, would probably be better than a larger but bare box. They will need a shelter, preferably filled with loose-packed hay or straw that they can burrow into, a water bottle, food dishes, and a log for gnawing.

Newspapers spread on the base of the tray will make a highly absorbent layer, but should be spread with a good floor litter such as peat moss or wood shavings.

A good, though less permanent, substitute for a wooden playpen is a 'train' of grocery cartons stuck together, and with guinea pig-sized openings cut from one to the other. Guinea pigs love tunnelling from one carton to another.

Feeding

Guinea pigs are by nature grazing animals and in the wild they live on the leaves, stems, and seeds of grasses and their associated plants. In captivity grass, hay, fresh vegetable matter and grain are all essential foodstuffs.

The use of an ark (pp.22-3) allows guinea pigs to graze safely each day, and is portable enough to be moved frequently to fresh areas of grass. If grass clippings are used they must be fed very fresh rather than left to ferment, and used only if quite free from chemicals, fertilizers, weed-killers, etc.

Plenty of top quality hay is invaluable to these animals, and should be offered in a hay rack to prevent it being trodden and soiled underfoot.

Many wild plants may also be fed to guinea pigs, who love such common weeds as groundsel and dandelion. Because some wild plants are poisonous, care must be taken not to offer any except those known to be safe (see opposite).

Raw fruit and vegetables help to satisfy the guinea pigs' particular need for a regular vitamin C intake.

Grass and hay are the single most important items in a guinea pig's diet. Good quality meadow hay is mainly green in colour, and sweet smelling, without any hint of mustiness. It is also free of harsh weeds such as thistle and dock.

WILD PLANT FOOD

Dandelion and groundsel are probably the two best known wild plants which are popularly fed to guinea pigs, but there are many more, found in lawns and weeded from flower beds, which can safely be added to their diet. These include: chickweed, clover, coltsfoot, cow parsley, shepherd's purse, sow thistle, vetch (many varieties) and yarrow.

Some plants, and leaves from certain trees, are unsuitable and often poisonous, including bindweed, bryony, buttercup (unless dried), dock, dog's mercury, foxglove, laburnum, nightshade (common and deadly), poppy, privet, ragwort, sorrel, traveller's joy (wild clematis), wild arum, wood anemone and yew.

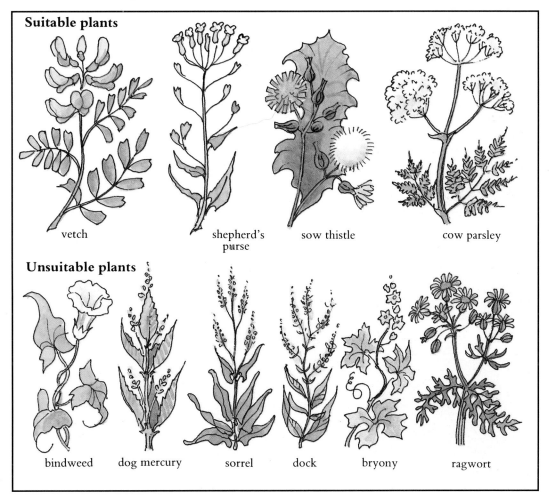

Suitable plants

vetch   shepherd's purse   sow thistle   cow parsley

Unsuitable plants

bindweed   dog mercury   sorrel   dock   bryony   ragwort

Guinea pigs enjoy lettuce, but too much can be as diuretic as too much dandelion.

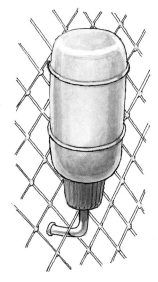

Water bottle

The food bowl should not tip over easily

Identification of wild plants can often be a problem, so it is better to play safe and feed only those plants which you positively know to be safe. Do not collect plants from hedgerows or fields and beware, too, of any plants which may have been on the receiving end of any chemicals.

Guinea pigs do not use their forefeet as hands, and so they feed better if the vegetables are cut into chunks.

Special treats include melon, with or without skin, or a stick of celery which will be dragged hastily into cover for solitary consumption, away from importunate companions.

Besides grass, hay, wild plants, and raw vegetables and fruit, guinea pigs also need some cereal food each day: crushed oats, proprietary grain mixture sold for guinea pigs, wholemeal bread, and possibly bran. This cereal compensates for the seeding grasses they would eat in the wild, and should be fed twice a day, either dry, or as a crumbly mash made with hot or cold milk or water. Bran should not be fed dry, but in a mash.

Remove mash bowls after feeding times to avoid left-over food going sour. Many guinea pigs have a habit of jumping into their food bowls, often contaminating the food with droppings, so frequent cleaning of the bowl is even more important.

Because feeding is a major activity of guinea pigs, fresh food needs to be available at all times, including night, when they need hay and vegetables.

The amount of water taken varies, particularly according to how much fresh food is available, but must always be within the guinea pigs' reach. Drip feed bottles need scouring to prevent the build-up of algae (see p.30).

Guinea pigs often chew their water bottles, so the spouts should not be plastic but metal, preferably stainless steel.

Useful food supplements include a mineral lick (bought from a pet shop); cod liver oil in winter; and, dissolved in the water, one 250 mg tablet of vitamin C (from the chemist).

Suggested diet chart

	What?	When?	How much?
Adult guinea pig	guinea pig mix from pet shop *or* mash *or* guinea pig pellets	morning and evening	as much as the guinea pig will eat at a 'sitting'
	mixed fresh greens washed in cold water	morning and evening	
	fresh water mineral lick hay	always available	
	whole apple carrot stick of celery melon (including skin) tomato	one of these items daily	
	vitamin C tablet	always available (in water bottle)	1×250mg tablet dissolved in water
Pregnant sow (during gestation period of 63 days)	As above, but gradually increase amounts as pregnancy progresses. Ensure sow is receiving sufficient by checking that a little is left at the end of each meal. (Remember to remove excess food.) Add a little milk to her diet.		
Nursing sow (during lactation and afterwards)	As above, slowly cutting back amount but returning to normal intake only several weeks after weaning.		
Growing young	Mixed diet as for adult, offered from two days old.		

Cleaning the hutch

It is said that one advantage of keeping guinea pigs, rather than some of the other rodent pets, is that they are odourless. This is true, but even so there will be an unpleasant smell if they are kept in a hutch that is not cleaned out for days on end. Flooring or floor litter saturated with urine, piles of faeces – even those deposited neatly in one corner, as many owners find – and decaying vegetables will soon make the hutch unhygienic.

A guinea pig's hutch in constant use must be cleaned out daily. This routine attention includes removing droppings, checking the floor litter is dry, and replacing that in the damp corner if necessary. One should tidy the sleeping compartment, make sure the amount of bedding is adequate for the weather conditions, replenish hay and other feedstuffs, and wash and refill the drip feed bottle.

Dirt collected in the drinking tube of the water bottle should be poked out with a small bottle brush. The bottle should be washed weekly in a mild detergent and rinsed well. Algae can be removed by bleach, followed by a *thorough* washing in detergent and water, and then a really good final rinse. A few drops of mild disinfectant (not phenol-based) sprinkled on the hutch floor before replenishing the litter will help keep away flies in hot weather.

When the animals spend most of their time outside in an enclosure or, if safety allows, free in the garden, then cleaning the hutch every other day may suffice. Even so, food, water, and bedding must be checked daily.

Periodically a hutch will need to be thoroughly cleaned and scrubbed, and allowed to dry completely before being used again. However, if serious disease strikes it is best to burn the hutch and start again with a different one.

Any concrete area in a permanent run should be hosed down from time to time. Nibbled-down grass within a portable run needs to be lightly dusted with lime and not re-used until it has completely regrown. The same patch should only be used two or three times a year to prevent stomach upsets.

Daily cleaning of the hutch will include removal of droppings, uneaten food and soiled litter, checking bedding is clean, and providing fresh hay and water.

Grooming

It is very important that rough-haired and long-haired varieties should be kept in good, sanitary conditions, or their hair is liable to become matted together in a most unpleasant way. Abyssinian, Peruvian and Sheltie varieties, together with rough or long-haired cross-breds, ought to be groomed daily. Brush the way the fur grows, using a stiff brush that will remove loose hairs, tangles, and pieces of twig, dry leaves or burrs that may have become enmeshed. Short-haired breeds should be brushed once a week with a baby's hairbrush. Gentle but firm insistence on grooming from a young age for all these breeds will gradually accustom them to it as a matter of routine. It will help keep them tame, and also afford the owner opportunity to observe their condition carefully, and take action if need be (pp.38-9).

Soft brush suitable for grooming

The coat will probably not often become very dirty, but if it does, or if the guinea pig is to be entered for a show, wash the animal down with a very mild soapy water or baby shampoo. The eyes and ears should be avoided and the coat rinsed thoroughly with warm water. Thorough drying with a towel is essential, though a hairdryer can be used, provided the animal is not frightened by the noise. To avoid a chill, the guinea pig should be kept warm indoors until it is absolutely dry. Shampooing in cold weather should, if at all possible, be avoided.

Grooming is a job especially for the owners of rough- and long-haired guinea pigs, but advisable with any breed.

Handling

Guinea pigs are quite the easiest of the pet rodents to handle, many being readily tamed and generally docile. They are unlikely to struggle or bite when picked up competently by their regular handler, but even so great care should be taken not to drop them. Because they are rather heavy for their size, and not as agile as other rodents, they are vulnerable to injury of the limbs or spine if dropped, even from a small height, or if they are subjected to rough handling. Guinea pigs are easily frightened by sudden movements so the handler should always move slowly and quietly, approaching the animal from the front and on the same level.

It is important that, particularly towards the end of her pregnancy, a gravid sow should be handled with great care and gentleness, and then only when necessary. There is some danger that the young could be still-born as a result of rough or excessive handling of their mother while they were in the womb.

The recommended way to lift a young guinea pig is with two hands – one around the hind quarters, to support the animal's weight, the other over the shoulders, to control the movement of the forelimbs. An adult guinea pig is best picked up with one hand supporting the hind quarters, the other around its chest.

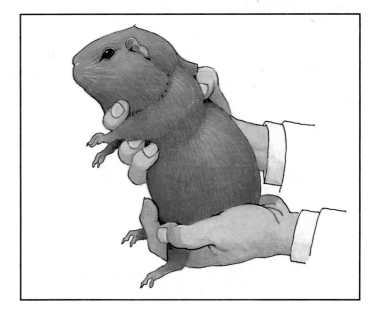

The healthy guinea pig

Cross-bred guinea pigs need as much care as pure-breds to keep them healthy.

Guinea pigs should live for between four and seven years or even longer, if they are bred from strong stock and are well-cared for in clean, spacious accommodation with protection from cold and damp, suitable food, plenty of exercise and somewhere to hide.

To make sure the guinea pigs keep healthy, look carefully at and handle them every day, so the first signs of anything wrong can easily be detected. It is important to know how a guinea pig looks when it is well; then it is easier to recognize quickly any change for the worse in its appearance and behaviour.

A guinea pig should be examined regularly and carefully, especially the ears, eyes, nose and sexual organs.

Always wash your hands thoroughly before feeding or handling any pet, but especially if disease is suspected.

Guinea pigs can catch colds from humans; if you have a cold you should stay away from the guinea pigs for a few days and get someone else to feed them.

When guinea pigs do fall ill, prompt veterinary attention is needed because, like many small animals, they deteriorate very quickly and have rather poor powers of recuperation. Warmth is essential. It should always be remembered that guinea pigs dehydrate extraordinarily rapidly, so the sufferer should be carefully drip fed with water through an eyedropper or a syringe without the needle.

Overgrown teeth Guinea pigs can be prone to overgrown teeth and their front or incisor teeth may need to be cut by a vet or person experienced in this. It is quickly done and will not hurt the guinea pig. Prevention, however, is better than cure, so the guinea pig should always have access to a gnawing block, preferably a newly cut log with the bark left on. Hard food, such as root vegetables and the stems of kale and Brussels sprouts, will help the wearing-down process.

Overgrown claws These can be trimmed with a nail clipper bought from a pet shop. It is often safer to watch a vet or experienced pet keeper clip the claws on the first occasion, after which it is not difficult to follow suit. The importance of having handled the guinea pig enough to make it docile for this exercise cannot be overstressed.

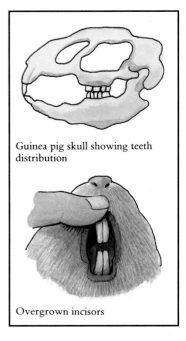

Guinea pig skull showing teeth distribution

Overgrown incisors

SIGNS OF HEALTH

Anus	clean, no staining or scouring
Appetite	good, eating frequently and during night
Breathing	silent and regular
Body	firm and well-fleshed, no growths, swellings or scaly skin
Claws	short and trim, no splits
Coat	clean, no soiling by faeces or urine; no tangles, skin eruptions, or parasites
Demeanour	alert, responsive and inquisitive, posture normal, not flattened
Droppings	small, elongated pellets about 1cm/½ in long
Ears	rose petal shaped, turning downwards, not torn, no discharge
Eyes	wide open and bright, no cloudiness or discharge
Feet	strong and well-formed, no soreness of hocks, weight distributed evenly
Mouth	clean, with no slobbering
Movement	rapid shuffling, close to the ground, and a 'trot' with body held high off the ground, freezes when alarmed
Nose	clear of any discharge or dried mucus
Teeth	worn down naturally on hard food and gnawing blocks

Even when you cannot be there, your guinea pigs will need their daily diet of mash or pellets, hay, water and fresh fruit and vegetables.

When you are away

Guinea pigs need attention every single day, so at holiday time they must either be boarded out with a knowledgeable person, or someone must come in daily with food and water. If the animals are in an outdoor enclosure or ark, they must be shut into their hutch at night. Someone must also be willing to clean the hutch out if the owner's absence is for longer than a few days. It is a good idea to leave a note by the hutch to confirm the type and quantity of food to give, a reminder to refill water bottles, etc. Adding the vet's telephone number is a wise precaution.

A small cat basket makes a good guinea pig carrier, but in an emergency a strong cardboard box, pierced for ventilation and with the top tied down securely, makes a good substitute.

First aid

In an emergency expert veterinary advice should be sought urgently, but it is important meanwhile to handle the guinea pig correctly and do the right thing to speed its treatment. Generally, the animal should be kept warm and prevented from dehydrating (p.35). When the guinea pig is very cold, a small drop of whisky is an invaluable reviver.

Accidents Probably for a suspected fracture the vet will want the guinea pig brought to the surgery rather than make a house call, so ask how to move the guinea pig safely, without aggravating its problem.

When a fracture is not suspected, the guinea pig should be picked up in the usual way, wrapped in an old towel for extra warmth, and taken immediately to the vet. A cardboard pet carrier, or a strong grocery box pierced with airholes and secured with a lid and string, makes a good conveyance. Some hay on top of a lining of absorbent newspaper will make it comfortable – and leakproof.

Heatstroke Confined to small, badly ventilated hutches or left in direct sunlight from which they cannot escape, guinea pigs are very prone to heatstroke. If an animal is found in obvious and acute distress, possibly in a state of collapse, its back must be wetted immediately with a damp cloth and the animal removed at once to a cool place with good ventilation. It should be fanned if severely affected.

An ear bitten in a fight, and bathing gently with a cotton bud dipped in saline solution.

Wounds Torn ears, sore hocks, and skin abrasion may be the result of keeping incompatible guinea pigs together. Consult a veterinary surgeon if the wound is serious, or becomes infected, but otherwise bath in a saline solution. Keep males apart, and separate females if they constantly fight and kick. Normally compatible guinea pigs may fight when overcrowded. Abscesses occur quite frequently as a result of a wound and must be lanced by the vet when they are ripe and 'cheesy'. The vet may also administer antibiotics.

Ailments and parasites

Bald patches   If starting on the face and looking pale and scaly, these may be caused by ringworm. Itchy patches may be a sign of mange. A bald patch in the middle of the back that neither spreads nor itches may be the result of an over-rich diet. Reduce pelleted food and offer more green-stuff and hay. If patches persist, seek veterinary advice.

Constipation   This may be due to disease, lack of rough-age, or too dry a diet (perhaps with too much cereal and pellet food), fed without sufficient water.

Diarrhoea   Diarrhoea may be due to an intestinal infec-tion, introduced by way of contaminated or frosted veg-etable matter, or due to a sudden change in diet. If it persists or occurs with other symptoms, advice should be sought.

Flystrike   Long-haired guinea pigs can suffer from the 'strike fly' which lays its eggs in faeces-soiled fur. Within 12 to 24 hours, maggots hatch out and eat their way into the animal's flesh, with fatal results. All guinea pigs should be checked daily to ensure their coats are faeces-free. Hutches should be cleaned and bedding changed daily.

Hair stripping   This abnormal behaviour, when guinea pigs strip their own hair as far as they can reach or strip each other, tends to occur in the long-haired breeds. Some young are made quite hairless in this way by their own parents. The cause may be boredom and, in particular, the lack of something to chew. This is one reason why it is essential to give guinea pigs as much hay as they will eat, and to keep them in pairs or small groups in as interesting an environment as possible.

Loss of balance   A guinea pig which holds its head to one side and which may veer round in circles, quite unable to walk in a straight line, is showing symptoms of middle ear disease and professional advice should be sought.

Frequent observation of your guinea pig's condition and behaviour is the best way to spot any health problem before it progresses too far.

Parasites Guinea pigs are usually free of parasites unless there are infected cats and dogs, for instance, in the house. They may, however, become infested with lice, perhaps from infected hay or straw. Either bath the guinea pig with a medicated shampoo or treat with a mild insecticide powder. Repeat the treatment once a week, and if in any doubt or difficulty, seek veterinary help.

Pseudotuberculosis Enlarged glands in the neck and growths in the abdomen may be caused by a serious condition known as pseudotuberculosis. Sometimes death is rapid, but variations of the condition may cause a slow deterioration in the guinea pig over several weeks. This is a highly infectious disease and veterinary advice must be sought.

Respiratory infections Symptoms similar to those associated with the common cold in man are made worse by poor living conditions, and can develop into **pneumonia**. Rehousing the guinea pigs in isolation in a dry, warm and roomy cage will often bring about an improvement and stop the spread of these respiratory infections. If in doubt, or if the symptoms persist, do not hesitate to seek veterinary advice.

Salmonellosis An organism of the salmonella group causes rapid loss of condition followed by collapse. This very serious disease has a high mortality rate and spreads quickly through large colonies. Veterinary attention is vital because the most rigorous cleaning and disinfecting is necessary before it is safe to introduce new stock into the accommodation after an outbreak. Animals that do survive an attack may act as carriers and cause subsequent outbreaks. There is also a hazard to human health, and therefore particular care over personal hygiene must be taken.

Vitamin C deficiency Guinea pigs, and especially pregnant sows, have a particular need for a high daily vitamin C intake. A deficiency may lead to scurvy, and a loss of resistance to other diseases. Pellets fed without a variety of fresh vegetables and fruit, or those prepared for other animals, may not contain enough vitamin C to meet this need. Guinea pigs not feeding adequately because of overgrown teeth (p.35) may not take in enough of the vitamin, even though the right foods are available to them.

Reproduction

A female guinea pig could well produce five litters a year. Finding good homes for so many offspring can be a major problem, so the golden rule about breeding from pet guinea pigs is: don't. Owners who want to breed from pure-breds would be well advised to join a good local Cavy Club and acquire a thorough background knowledge before beginning.

As a general rule it is inadvisable to breed from young females of any species who may have reached puberty but who are too immature in behaviour to deal with their own young patiently and competently. The same applies if they are too physically immature for the pelvis to have reached an adequate size to prevent pain and difficulty (dystocia) during the birth process.

The case of the guinea pig is rather different. There may be a greater risk of dystocia if the guinea pig does not have her first litter while she is still young. Once fully grown, the pelvic bones fuse, leaving her with a rigid, perhaps under-sized pelvis, and this may cause difficult births and a shorter breeding span than normal.

For this reason it is recommended that guinea pigs should be mated at a relatively young age, maybe as early as 12 weeks. The litter will then be born before the mother reaches full maturity, and before the two halves of the pelvis fuse firmly together. However, with a sow slow to mature it may be advisable for her not to breed before she is six months old. A vet would have to advise on individual cases. Subsequent births should be trouble-free.

Many females first mated when very young breed successfully and easily beyond the age of 18-24 months, which is usually quoted as the time to retire guinea pigs from breeding. Even so, it is advisable, as always, to retire the older stock from breeding to make way for younger and more vigorous animals to continue a healthy line.

So it is better if the boar and sow are separated for periods, to avoid the chances of pregnancy. In particular, many owners find it advisable to house a pregnant sow alone for a week or two before her litter is due, because she needs very careful handling and quiet conditions then, and leave her alone to bring up her family until weaning age. If the boar were left with the sow she would be likely to become pregnant again immediately after giving birth.

Pregnant females drink thirstily and will take milk as well as water. Their diet must be increased to support the unborn or suckling young (see p.29) and if there are more than three in the litter they will need extra milk since she has only two mammary glands.

It has already been said that guinea pigs are intolerant of low temperatures, and are liable to suffer heat exhaustion. A heavily pregnant sow is particularly vulnerable in this respect. If she is kept in a hutch it must be moved to a shady position and hosed with cold water.

Mother suckling young

The young

The delightful young of the guinea pig are born with a full coat, with their eyes open, their teeth already cut, able to move around – supporting their weight on their legs – and attempting to take solid food within a day or two.

This exceptional maturity at birth makes them the loveliest of all the usual pet rodent babies. They are born after a long gestation of about 63 days, usually in rather small litters, and single births are not uncommon. Average birth weight for the females is 85g/3oz; 90g/3½oz for the males. Single birth weights may be as much as 150g/5¼oz.

Because they are so well-developed, there is very little likelihood of new-born guinea pigs being at risk from their parents, as is the case with mice, rats, rabbits, and gerbils.

It is very tempting to show off such enchanting youngsters to friends and family, but this should be resisted for a few days. The owner should, however, check there are no dead or sickly young, and that all are suckling well.

Suckling continues for about three weeks, but the young are best left with the sow until the age of four or five weeks when they weigh perhaps 250g/8½oz. There is no danger in leaving both sow and boar with the young to live as a small colony, although of course there is the risk of the sow becoming pregnant again.

The young are not able to mate each other before the males reach puberty at 8-10 weeks, although in a family group the females would be at risk of being mated by their father once they reached puberty at perhaps 4-5 weeks. They should, therefore, be separated from their father before this age. Segregation into sexes should take place at about six weeks, and it may also be necessary then to separate individual boars to prevent fighting.

These are social animals, and if they are rehomed at the age of eight weeks, it is very unfair to expect them to live a solitary life in captivity. For this reason the females are most often recommended as pets, since they will usually live peaceably in small groups of two or more.

Guinea pigs have an enduring reputation as one of the

most successful pet animals and for their agreeable natures. The long-haired breeds need some extra attention, by way of daily grooming, but all are fairly simple to care for if their accommodation has been well thought out in advance, and proves adequate in severe weather, and if the very necessary chore of frequent cleaning out is not too daunting a task.

Young guinea pigs, being perfect miniatures of their parents, are truly enchanting babies.

Your questions answered

My guinea pigs are very fond of chewing their water bottles. They have ruined several already. How can I stop them?

To stop your guinea pigs breaking their drinking bottle by gnawing, buy a bottle with a metal spout, and fix it securely to the outside of the cage. For preference, the metal should be stainless steel, as aluminium is softer and a determined guinea pig can ultimately succeed in piercing it. Giving the animals plenty of hard things to gnaw on should switch their attention away from gnawing the spout.

Check also that the water is flowing satisfactorily through the spout. Some guinea pigs are thirsty little creatures and it could be they are having difficulty drawing enough water down through the spout.

My guinea pigs seem prone to skin infections. Is there anything I can do to prevent this?

A skin infestation by a small mite, similar to that which causes mange in other animals, is a scourge to many guinea pigs. Most carry the mite, but it usually only shows itself in animals that are less than fully fit, elderly, pregnant or nursing.

The mange causes violent itching and scratching, raw skin from the scratching, and usually a serious loss of weight. A vet can prescribe a suitable skin bath (to be used at precisely regular intervals for effectiveness). If several guinea pigs live together, all must be treated, even though only one has the problem. The whole cage and run must also be thoroughly cleaned.

Should my guinea pigs be encouraged to exercise? Compared with my very active hamster, they seem to lead a very sedentary existence.

Guinea pigs are not as regularly on the move as hamsters and certainly do not need an exercise wheel, for instance. But they will be quite active at certain times of the day if they are given sufficient interesting things to do. A really spacious run, or secure part of the garden, with lots of cover, tunnels, etc will demonstrate that in a natural state guinea pigs run about a great deal – in fact their wild relatives are called restless cavies. But a guinea pig confined only to its hutch, with no toys or 'adventure playground', will be bored and probably not exercise much.

How often should a guinea pig's claws be clipped?
As often as necessary, depending on how hard the surface is on which the animal exercises. Check the claws over at least once a week.

What are Dalmatian guinea pigs?
Rather like Dalmatian dogs – spotted black on a white background.

I was very disappointed when my pure-bred pair of Himalayan guinea pigs produced a litter of white youngers, with no colourpoints. What has gone wrong?
Nothing – All Himalayans are born like that. Wait two or three weeks and the points will start to darken until the guinea pigs get their full coloration at around the age of six months.

Is it safe for guinea pigs to eat runner bean leaves?
There is no evidence to suggest that runner bean leaves are poisonous to guinea pigs, so it should be quite safe to feed them this greenstuff. However, the beans themselves can be toxic if eaten raw, so the guinea pigs should not be given access to runner bean plants.

I have seen my guinea pig eating its own droppings. Should I stop it doing this, and if so, how?
Coprophagy, or eating of an animal's own droppings, is normal for guinea pigs, and is similar to cows chewing the cud. The guinea pig is not eating the hard droppings from the floor of the hutch, but small, moist droppings which it takes directly from its anus. The protein content of these is essential for the animal's health.

Potential owners should be told about this habit (which is also indulged in by the rabbit), otherwise many parents may worry unnecessarily or even have the guinea pigs destroyed, mistakenly thinking that the animals will transmit disease to their children.

Life history

Scientific name	*Cavia porcellus*
Gestation period	63 days (approx.)
Litter size	2–4 (average)
Birth weight	85–90g about 3oz (average)
Eyes open	at birth
Weaning age	21–28 days
Weaning weight	about 250g/8½oz
Puberty	males 8–10 weeks females 4–5 weeks
Adult weight	males 1000g/35oz females 850g/30oz
Best age to breed	12 weeks (see p.40)
Oestrus (or season)	every two weeks (approx.)
Duration of oestrus	15 hours (approx.)
Retire from breeding	2 years (see p.41)
Life expectancy	4–7 years

Record card

Record sheet for your own guinea pigs

<table>
<tr><td>(photograph or portrait)</td><td>(photograph or portrait)</td></tr>
</table>

Name _____

Date of birth
(actual or estimated) _____

Variety _____ Sex _____

Colour/description _____

Name _____

Date of birth
(actual or estimated) _____

Variety _____ Sex _____

Colour/description _____

Feeding notes _____
_____
_____
_____
_____
_____
_____
_____

Medical notes _____
_____
_____
_____
_____
_____
_____
_____

Veterinary surgeon's name _____

Practice address _____
_____

Surgery hours _____
_____
_____

Tel. no. _____

Index

Abscesses, 37
Abyssinian, 6, 7, 9, 14, 17, 32
Agouti, 6, 7, 8, 9
Ailments, 38-9
American, 6, 9
Ark, 22-3, 26

Balance, loss of, 38
Bald patches, 38
Bedding, 20, 30
Biology, 12-13
Bolivian, 6, 9, 19
Boredom, 25, 38
Breathing, 14, 35. *See also* Respiratory infections
Breeding, 14-15, 40

Carriers, 36, 37
Cavia cutleri, 10
Cavia porcellus, 4, 10
Cavy, 4, 10-11
Cavy clubs, 4, 9, 40
Choosing, 14
Claws, 13, 35
Cold weather, 5, 21, 24
Colouring, 6-8, 45
Companionship, 5, 16
Constipation, 38
Coronet, 9

Dehydration, 35, 36
Diarrhoea, 14, 38
Diet, imbalance in, 38

Droppings, 28, 30, 35, 45
Dutch, 7
Dystocia, 40

Ears, 14, 35, 38
Enclosure, 20-1, 30
English, 6, 9
Exercise, 22-3, 24-5, 44-5
Eyes, 14, 35, 47

Feeding, 26-9, 37
Fighting, 5, 16, 37
First aid, 37
Flystrike, 38

Gestation, 12, 42, 47
Gnawing block, 12, 25, 35, 44
Grazing, 22-3, 26, 30
Grooming, 4, 15, 32

Hair, stripping, 38
Handling, 14, 16, 33, 35
Health, 14, 34-5
Heat, protection from, 22, 37, 41
Heredity, 6
Himalayan, 7, 8, 45
Holidays, 36
Hutches, 20-1, 30-1
Hygiene, 28-9, 30-1, 34, 38, 39
Hystricomorpha, 12

Lice, 39
Long-haired breeds, 4, 6, 9, 15, 32, 43

Marked (colouring), 6-8, 9
Mating, 40-1
Middle ear disease, 38
Mineral lick, 29
Myomorpha, 12

Parasites, 39
Peruvian, 6, 9, 15, 19, 32
Play pen, 24-5
Poison, 12, 26, 27, 45
Pregnancy, 12, 29, 33, 41, 42
Pseudotuberculosis, 39

Reproduction, 40-1
Respiratory infections, 34, 39
Ringworm, 38
Rosettes, 6, 9
Rough-haired breeds, 6, 8, 9, 14, 15, 18, 32

Salmonellosis, 39
Sciuromorpha, 12
Self (colouring), 6, 8, 9
Sexing, 15
Sheltie, 9, 32
Short-haired breeds, 4, 6, 8, 9, 15
Skin condition, 14, 44

Sources, 9, 15
South America, guinea pigs in, 4, 5, 6, 10-11, 12

Tail, 13
Teeth, 12, 14, 35, 39
Temperament, 4, 16, 33
Tortoiseshell, 7, 8, 9, 17
Tortoiseshell and White, 5, 6, 8, 9, 18

Varieties, 6-9
Vitamin C, 26, 29, 39
Voice, 12

Water, 28-9, 44
Wild plants, as food, 26, 27-8
Wounds, 37

Young, the, 10, 14, 18, 29, 41, 42-3